Interior Design in Miniature

BROOKE TUCKER ORIGINALS

By Anne Day Smith

Interior Design in Miniature

BROOKE TUCKER ORIGINALS

By Anne Day Smith

Boynton and Associates, Inc.
Clifton, Virginia

Printed in the United States of America, by Benton Review Printing. Edited by
Sybil Harp. Cover and inside page design by Jack Gordon. Art production by Jan Crerie.

All photographs are by Bruce Bucell or Don Cadette, with the exception of the Cabbage
Rose Room pictured on page 33, which was photographed by Bonnie Schroeder. The
photograph on page 37 of the full-size room at Hillwood was provided by the
Hillwood Museum.

In loving memory
of my father, Harry L. Day,
who long ago instilled in me a love of books and encouraged
my first attempts at writing.

❦ Acknowledgements ❦

The Author wishes to acknowledge and thank the following people who have been an integral part of this project:

Brooke Tucker, the subject of this book, whose genuine warmth and vitality, honesty and outgoing personality, have made this a truly enjoyable and exciting project.

Sybil Harp, the Editor, whose enthusiastic commitment to the project from its inception has never waned, and whose professional expertise has been invaluable.

And special thanks to my in-house editor, husband and best friend, Gerry Smith.

The Editor would like to thank the following people who assisted in the production of this book:

Chris Harris of International Scanner Corporation of America for his knowledgeable advice and careful attention to the separation of the color photographs.

Julie Lancaster, Advertising Manager of *Nutshell News,* for making phone calls, writing ad copy, preparing late ads, and in countless other ways filling in for me so that I could have time to devote to this project; and Bonnie Schroeder, Editor of *Nutshell News,* for her helpful suggestions and assistance.

Jeanne Pearson and Irene Day of the Production Department of Boynton and Associates, who were never too busy to stop what they were doing and lend a hand when I needed it.

Except where noted, all of the rooms shown in this book are, to the best of our knowledge, in private collections.

❧ Contents ❧

❧ Introduction ❧

Fascination with small objects has occupied mankind since the dawn of civilization. It has evolved to the point where, today, miniatures are considered a highly respected art form. They are collected, displayed, and cherished in much the same way we collect paintings or sculpture. As with these other art forms, our collections of miniature objects are personal reflections of our own tastes, interests, and aspirations.

Through our collections we can live in another dimension, possibly a different time period, certainly a more controllable existence than the real life surrounding us. In miniature, anything is possible.

Interior design in miniature is meant to be viewed in much the same way a fine painting or object of sculpture would be viewed, as a whole, not as a combination of its various parts. A miniature room combines the artistic significance of a fine painting with the three-dimensional aspects of an object of sculpture. But, it is as variable and diverse as any other art form. Ideally, a miniature room is displayed set into a wall, framed as a painting would be, yet taking the viewer one step further, attracting him to more closely examine the nuances of its three-dimensional properties.

Interior designers who work in miniature approach their projects as painters or sculptors do, creating miniature environments to please our visual senses, bringing together colors and textures to create a unified whole.

The principles of interior design apply to miniature rooms just as they do to rooms in real size. Each must have harmony, rhythm, a sense of balance, and taste and imagination.

Taste can be cultivated by one's exposure to the best in art. Imagination, too, can be cultivated in much the same way. Imagination in interior design suggests the ability to use borrowed ideas and adapt them in new ways. In this regard interior design in miniature, and the rooms shown in this book in particular, can be adapted to many real size situations.

Like every other art form, interior design has basic principles that must be learned. Students in design classes learn these basics by constructing miniature rooms as part of their curriculum. Miniature rooms are also used by professional interior designers to demonstrate graphically to clients how their own real size rooms might look once the decorating project is completed.

It is not unusual for a designer of miniature rooms to be asked to perform this task. Starting with the dimensions of a room, and the client's color preferences, the interior designer installs architectural details, incorporates color and texture, creates an environment often dramatically different from what might have existed in that space.

To be successful, interior design in miniature must combine a flair for the dramatic and theatrical, with those more disciplined ingredients we normally associate with good design.

It is this combination we see in Brooke Tucker's rooms, this flair and discipline that sets her work apart, and makes it so special. The fascination with small objects continues today.

**Look for a long time at what
pleases you...**
—*Collette*

"When I was creating this room, I realized I wanted to do something a little different. I had the beige and white paper, and I laid out the floor plan. I wanted that to look different, too. When I found that turquoise/aqua fabric, something went 'bing' in my head: that would look great with the paper.

"It's a room I'm very happy with. It's very stylized, as a lot of my work is. It is very severe in its way, although it has a softness to it, too. When I did it, it gave me a totally satisfied feeling."

—*Brooke Tucker*

"**I** adore pink roses," Brooke declares, "and whenever I can, I use them." This is a wide, open room that would be 30 feet in length if it were real size, from the sitting area with grand piano on the right, to the bathroom on the left.

"Most of my bedrooms are bedrooms with bath," she explains. The bathroom, however, does not contain a toilet. "They are not necessary in the scheme of things," Brooke believes. "They don't make a room prettier." She seldom uses toilets in her miniature bathrooms.

Dreams are the touchstones of our characters.

—Henry David Thoreau

Sometimes an architectural detail or a piece of
furniture will provide the idea for one of Brooke's
rooms. In this case, it was an antique cabinet with a
simple crown that she saw in a shop.

"I liked it so much a whole room popped into my
head," she recalls, "and I thought, I wonder if I can
do that."

This bedroom, with its bath/dressing room, has a
definitely traditional feeling, but still retains the
"Brooke" look. The antique cabinet has been adapted
and used in the rear right side of the bath/dressing
room. It has a mirrored door, and Brooke has carried
the crown molding detail along the back of the room
where she has placed a second built-in cupboard.

"I am especially pleased with the figurines and the
built-in case they are in," Brooke says. "Those are
Prieser figures from Germany." She changed the
groupings of the figures by re-positioning parts of them,
then handpainted each, even including details such as
eyelashes. "I did what I've never done before in those
figurines," she continues, "and I wanted a cabinet to
highlight them."

The figurine cabinet is built into the wall on the
bedroom side of this room setting, sharing a light
source with the dressing table behind it in the bath
area.

"That fabric," Brooke explains, "happens to be a
seafoam green and beige, but I found it in many
different colors and it's a joy to work with. It is a
tailored fabric, but I have used it in a very feminine
room, too. And it works!"

One's only real life is the life one never leads.
—Oscar Wilde

A *Fairy Princess bedroom is how Brooke describes this room because the woodwork, and even some of the furniture, is finished in a bright gold leaf.*

The aqua fabric used throughout is covered with white lace, "almost embossed," she explains, adding that "it is very hard to get lace that I feel is in scale." Additional color in the room is provided by a very fine European lace trim embroidered with pink roses which Brooke has set into vertical panels on the walls.

This room is on display at Angel's Attic in Santa Monica, California, a non-profit museum of antique dollhouses, miniatures, dolls and toys, which is sponsored by the Angels for Autistic Children for the benefit of Brentwood Center for Educational Therapy.

Founder-Director Jackie McMahan told Brooke the room is a favorite of the children who visit the museum, and that it is displayed at their eye level. "She told me the little children stand there mesmerized," Brooke says, pleased that this room is bringing joy to so many.

*T*ypically *"Brooke,"* this bathroom is elegant and stylized. And contains no toilet because *"my mythical people don't need them,"* she laughs.

Although its size cannot be determined by these photographs, Brooke describes this as a *"huge room, and the first time I used a double fireplace, separating the room by a fireplace that opens into both sides."* One fireplace faces the foot of the bed. The other fireplace is out of our view, to the right, in the sitting area of this bedroom.

Soft gold woodwork complements the dusty rose fabric used in this room. Brooke considers this color *"so soft, so subtle,"* and explains that this is one of the many times she has used a bridal theme. *"That's why,"* she goes on, *"you'll see the mannequin with the bride's veil in the bath, and on the other side of this room her wedding gown is hanging on the closet door."* The bridal theme is a Brooke Tucker favorite. *"I don't know why,"* she says with a sigh, *"probably some unfulfilled dream I have."*

A small section of a much larger bedroom and bath features the table and chair set at left, decorated with strawberries and bows by Karen Markland, one of many artisans whose work Brooke admires. ''She is a terribly talented human being,'' Brooke declares. ''I saw some of the early things she did and got very excited, and her work has improved since.''

Brooke envisioned a room with a strawberries theme when she commissioned Karen to do these pieces. ''I told her I wanted something for the patio, totally ornate, totally carried away,'' Brooke says, recalling her excitement with the idea. ''That's the look I wanted.''

Brooke built the patio which is framed by a green and white striped awning and side curtains, as well as the walk and lawn with its flower border.

The mirror, which can be seen through the window, is also by Karen Markland. Brooke usually asks the artisan whose work she plans to use, ''to send me some companion pieces that I can use if I need them.'' Brooke handpainted the strawberries on a breakfast set made by Jo Parker.

All happiness depends on a leisurely breakfast.
—*John Gunther*

Until several years ago, "I worked exclusively in boxes," Brooke explains, "wooden boxes with frames on the front so they could be set into the walls of a customer's home." Then she attended a trade show and happened to see a miniature room built into a glass case. "I thought it was such a great look," she recalls, "so I had some glass cases built and started to work with them."

This room was the first in a series of three that Brooke created using this idea. The room can be viewed from three sides as well as from the top where there are glass panels above the bedroom and above the patio beyond. Only the back wall is not meant to be viewed since it provides space for electricity for the bedside and table lamps. A scene outside the windows on either side of the bed gives added visual interest.

Claiming that she doesn't usually favor angels and cupids, Brooke says, "I don't know why I used them in this room, but when I was making the headboard, they just seemed to work." She built the headboard of many smaller parts, handpainting the result in the same soft pastels she had used in the room's main color scheme.

Pointing out one pillow on the bed, the oblong one with rounded ends, Brooke confides, "that is actually not a pillow," explaining that it came from a shop in London's Portobello Road, and was originally the bow on a lady's blouse. "And the fringe around the bottom edge of the bedspread is the silk fringe and netting I removed from the same blouse," she explains.

Infinite riches in a little room.
—*Christopher Marlowe*

"**H**ere are the pink roses again,"
Brooke says with a smile suggesting that
her viewers are aware by now of how
much she likes them. "This is
upholstery fabric on the walls and, in
some people's eyes, I used a very strange
combination here — the rust-colored
cotton with this very European
upholstery fabric. But," she adds, "I
loved the two together, and I just went
with it."

Her innate sense of flair and creativity
is evident in this room she considers "a
retreat." Brooke confesses that "I don't
like clutter and I don't like things out of
place. This is the way I want to live."

The cat by Jan Yinger sitting on the
couch is so realistic, Brooke feels, "she
looks as if she's going to jump down
and go somewhere else."

If life is a Circus...

..,.Brooke Tucker deserves to be
there in the center ring. She is the
juggler who can funnel her creative
energies into several projects at once.
She is the entertainer whose sharp wit is
the delight of her friends, and of those
lucky enough to participate in her workshops. She is the ringmaster, seeing the
performance as a whole and inspiring
others to play their part.

Brooke's niche in the miniature world
is undisputed. Her work is recognized,
sought after, admired. Her creativity is
constantly emerging as each project
presents new challenges, new ways to
achieve that perfect effect.

A Brooke Tucker room seldom
evolves. It is there, in her mind, visually
complete. The project is often triggered
by a piece of fabric or wallpaper she
might see, and the whole room simply
becomes real, in her mind. At least,
that's the way Brooke explains it.

Brooke Tucker loves to talk — about

Brooke grew up in Hollywood. Movie studio back lots were her summer playgrounds. Her mother was an Earl Carroll showgirl before marrying Brooke's father, Forrest Tucker, a well-known actor.

Her parents divorced when Brooke was six. She lived with her mother during the school year, and spent summers with her father. It was then that she was allowed to wander by herself in the studios where he was working. She much preferred the quiet back lots to the busy sound stages. "I remember wandering down those back streets, seeing those houses. They weren't real," she knew, "but they looked real." The experience made a lasting impression on her. "That's very much the way I work," Brooke explains. "It's all a facade; the back of a room is never to be viewed, just like in the movies."

Brooke attended many different schools during her teen years, enjoying few of them, under duress in some cases, before she finally convinced her parents that her educational needs would be better served if she and her current school parted company for good.

It was with delight and a definite sense of adventure that she joined her father who was heading a road company production of *The Music Man*. She served the production company in a variety of capacities before beginning to work on the stage herself. She and her father toured together in several productions after that, and Brooke continued to work in the entertainment industry for several years. One of her favorite roles was that of Nurse Peerwood in the television series, *Medical Center*.

Brooke was often in front of a camera during her growing up years when her father, Forrest Tucker, was beginning his career as a popular movie actor. She frequently was taken to visit him at various filming locations, from the time she was a baby until she was in high school.

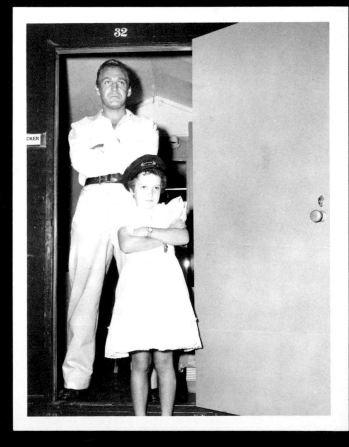

On location during the filming of "Medical Center" starring
Chad Everett, shown here in the driver's seat of the car. Brooke
wearing a shoulder-length wig, stands on the sidewalk with other
members of the crew.

The next few years found Brooke living on her own, first in Pittsburgh, then in Boston, working at an office job she did not enjoy very much, before being married in Boston. Shortly thereafter, she and her husband returned to Los Angeles to live. Their only child, a daughter, was born. But marriage and real life were not what Brooke expected them to be. Problems arose, conflicts developed and intensified.

Then, about a dozen years ago, Brooke reached a turning point in her life. Her marriage was over. Her daughter, Sandra, was living with her grandmother in Boston. Brooke moved into an apartment of her own, where she still lives, in Burbank, California.

Although she claims not to be an outwardly religious person, she firmly believes that she had the guidance of a Supreme Being at that point in her life, and that He — she calls Him "Ralph" — guided her into the miniature world.

"Ralph is a name I'm a lot more comfortable with," Brooke declares. "I honestly believe that twelve years ago, God took a look at me and said, 'We've got to get her some help. We must find her something to do or she's going to be a perpetual problem for us.' " She explains it in such a matter-of-fact way that you must believe that is exactly how it happened.

"And miniatures just appeared," Brooke continues. "I'd never heard of them before. They were just there, all of a sudden. It's got to have been that some other power, some other Somebody, found this for me."

Of course, the creativity was already there, inside her. "But I didn't know it," Brooke claims. "I will take credit for the work because I'm very disciplined in my work, probably because I love it, but I can't take credit . . . I mean, it just appeared. There it was for me to go for. It's always been a miracle to me."

Miniatures channeled the direction of her life from that moment on. "I do love this business," Brooke says. "I like getting up in the morning. I punch my own time clock, my mental time clock." Her boss is her public, the people who appreciate and buy her rooms.

Brooke's acting career began when she toured with her father in stage productions.

Recognition of her work came early.

She was one of the first to create contemporary miniature rooms, and to do them with a flair that has never diminished. Just the opposite, in fact.

"I never know what I'm going to do until I start working," Brooke explains. The mental image is there, but no one can view her work in progress and visualize the final result as is possible with the work of artisans in some other areas of miniatures. Because "the things aren't there," Brooke explains. Some of the "things" she is referring to are fillers and some are the focal points that tell the story.

Brooke's rooms do tell a story, or capture a moment in time. The time is now, today. "I wish I had lived in another time," Brooke says somewhat wistfully, "a prettier, more gracious time. But my work is not from an earlier time." Although many of her ideas stem from earlier periods in the history of interior design, "I take the look of them and adapt them, change them into *my* look of today," she explains. "I do 'Brooke.' I just do what seems right to me, although I've done a lot of rooms that give you the feeling of period rooms."

Besides creating a feeling, a moment in time, or telling a story, Brooke's rooms are recognizable because they carry the stamp of her personality. "I don't believe," she says, "that people have just one part to their personality." As the various segments of Brooke's personality come into her creative processes, she is able to construct very different types of rooms. She might create an unmistakably masculine room and then follow it with one that is decidedly feminine. "But they are both *my* rooms," she explains. Both types evolve from different parts of her personality, her creativity.

What her rooms all seem to have in common, though, is her sense of the dramatic, her flair for the theatrical. She admits that they are often "busy," that they are not the sort of rooms one actually lives in, although the people who love them wish they *could* live in them. "If a decorator did one of my rooms in real size," Brooke laughs, "she'd be out of business in a week."

What Brooke creates, then, is a fantasy in a miniature world where fantasies can be real, almost practical, and entirely possible.

"I'm simply not a realist," Brooke states about her work. "It's all very stylized, very fantasy-oriented, the way I'd like my life to look or to be." Even when there is a great deal of activity suggested in one of her rooms, there is that stylized, fantasy feeling because "everything matches," she explains. All of the accessories, the fillers as well as the focal points, are carefully chosen for their color, their texture, their relationship to each other and to the whole.

When Brooke begins working on one of her rooms, she thinks of it, technically, as a box, not just the room itself, but its components as well. "I am honestly convinced," she says, "that everything is basically a box, at least in 90% of the cases. If you can start with a structure such as a box, you can build anything. Your imagination tells you what to put in that box. It's such a simple concept that there's nothing you can't do."

It is this ability to put her concept into simple terms, and to convey it with such enthusiasm, that makes her workshops so popular. In the classes she conducts all over the country, Brooke teaches her students, first of all, how to design a room.

The three rooms shown on these pages illustrate not only the diversity of Brooke's work, but also the unity that exists within each room. The overall feeling of the wicker patio/dining area opposite is crisp, cool and casual. The "Strawberry Short-cake" child's room above, decorated in pink, red and green, conveys a spirit of playfulness, while the delicate bridal bedroom at left is a total expression of the feminine facet of its creator's personality.

"You know," she confides, "in twelve years I have still not found a better way, and I'm not saying there isn't one. But the way I do it," she says, her voice rising, "I like. It's simple, it makes sense to me because I'm not a technical person."

So, for Brooke, the technical part of designing a room begins, simply, with a blank sheet of paper the size of the floor space she plans to fill. With a pencil she sketches in the location of a window, a door, or some other architectural detail.

"Walls," she believes, "are just to hold the room together. I put a wall wherever I want it to be, whether it intersects another wall, whether it's something to look behind, I let my eyes do the feeling. If it looks right to my eye, I do it."

Brooke builds her walls of illustration board and wood bracing. "None of my walls are built of wood," she explains. "You just can't do with wood what you can do with board. You can do really interesting things with board as long as it is braced very well."

Brooke constructs the three walls of her rooms as separate units before installing them into their permanent locations. And the fourth wall? "I never see it," she claims. "In my mind, it's not there. This is a stage setting," Brooke believes. "The viewer is the fourth wall."

That fourth wall is also "my excuse if something is missing from a room, Brooke confides, amused. "If someone says, where is the . . ., I say, oh, it's behind you."

To decide on furniture placement, Brooke uses mock furniture, sample pieces that suggest the sizes and shapes of the items she will construct for the finished room. Using this mock furniture she can establish the spaciousness of the room.

Although she had already chosen the main color scheme of the room when she found the fabric or wallpaper that triggered her original idea, sometimes that idea "just keeps changing and the room takes on a character all its own as I'm working," she believes.

Brooke chooses the accessories "the same day I find the fabric for a new room. I'll color-pick things that have the feeling I want and put those aside," she explains, "and then I'll go through those and decide what will be going on in the room." She also selects some food which, like every other component in a Brooke Tucker room, is color- and texture-coordinated to the whole.

"All this," she claims, "is usually before I put a pencil to that blank piece of paper. I'm very disorganized in my life," Brooke admits, although many creative people are, "but I'm totally organized in my work."

In the next few weeks she will work on that room and "just create like a crazy person," she laughs.

The final result will be, as it has been for a dozen years, what you see on these pages— a Brooke Tucker Original.

A Brooke Tucker room in progress shows how she constructs the inner walls before putting them into the room, often selecting accessories to give her a feeling for the completed project.

"**I** *always really loved the cabbage rose look,*" *Brooke says, recalling bedroom wallpaper in a similar pattern during her growing up years. She was conducting a workshop in North Carolina, staying with a friend who had just acquired a piece of wicker with a cushion covered in this fabric. Brooke and her friend spent a day tracking down the fabric in local shops because Brooke liked it so much. "I fell in love with the pattern," she says.*

That fabric became the focal point of this room, or as Brooke laughs, "I was going to go overboard with cabbage roses, prayed I wasn't getting too far gone, and I just started working."

To continue the formal, yet country, feeling of the fabric, Brooke used dark woodwork and architectural detail in the hand-routed arches seen throughout the room. "It has the warmth of country," she believes. "It says so many things."

The portrait above the fireplace was cut from a magazine, a portrait artist's advertisement. "I go through these magazines constantly," Brooke confides, "and I just knew that was going to be right for this room."

Of the needlepoint work stand in front of the fireplace, Brooke says, "I am immensely proud of it because I didn't think I could make something like that." She copied the stand from a photograph, which is difficult to begin with, adding some work in progress to the 60-count silk gauze she installed on the stand. "I actually needlepointed a rose with a stem and leaves on it," Brooke says, proudly. "When that piece was done, I sat there for an hour just looking at it."

This completed room is one of Brooke's favorites. "I'm just so thrilled with this room. To me, it's romantic, it's feminine, it has my favorite pink roses. It embodies all of the things in my fantasy, in my mind."

Believing that particular breeds of dogs belong in certain types of rooms, Brooke explains: "Usually I use a masculine dog, like this Great Dane, in a masculine room, but when I finished this bedroom, I tried a feminine dog in it and it just didn't work."

The elegance of the room, she felt, required this breed of dog. "The minute I set that dog in there," Brooke continues, "I said, that's it! And, usually that's the way I make my decisions."

Brooke calls the colors in this room "very dusty, a pink-beige almost," and she created the elegant, almost royal, feeling of the room by using very soft, antique laces she found in Portobello Road in London. "I bought pieces," Brooke says, "and cut them up in different ways," using some of it as edging on the bed coverings.

The walls are covered in a lace fabric

Brooke has embellished using a method of French handsewing called "entre deux." The pink ribbon is strung through what originally was a solid piece of fabric because Brooke took the time to "clip every other teeny, little circle all the way up and down those walls," with a pair of manicure scissors. "You probably think," Brooke laughs, "oh, that ought to have been quick, but it nearly drove me mad."

The painting above the fireplace was originally a card Brooke found in England and, she explains, "I hand-painted it to match this room." The card's colors were lavenders which Brooke decided just would not "work" in this room. the photo on the dressing table is a picture of minaturists Joe and Janet Hermes' daughter Heidi, and her husband Dave Hart, taken on their wedding day.

"I like this room very much," Brooke confides. It's delicate."

Hillwood

When she was in Washington, D.C., in 1980 to attend the N.A.M.E. (National Association of Miniature Enthusiasts) National Houseparty, Brooke called ahead for an appointment to visit Hillwood, the former estate of the late Marjorie Merriweather Post, which is maintained as a museum and open to the public.

Brooke had developed a strong interest in the history of pre-revolutionary Russia, and especially in the last of the Romanovs, Nicholas II, his czarina Alexandra Fedorovna, and their court jeweler, Peter Carl Faberge. She knew the Post Faberge collection at Hillwood was legendary, and was anxious to see it.

Brooke toured the house in awe. "It was so palatial," she recalls, "and it was not within my ability, at the time, to create most of the rooms in that house. They were simply much too much."

But there was one room she knew would lend itself perfectly to a vignette. "Off the major dining room," she explains, "is a breakfast room. It just seemed like a simple, little room set off from all that splendor." That was the room she chose to reproduce, and she used photographs of it as her guide.

The Sevres porcelain on the table is an exact copy of the original, and Brooke handpainted the carpeting in the vignette to match the original. From a brochure she brought home after the tour, Brooke cut a scene of the estate's lawn and gardens as it would have been viewed from the breakfast room window, and installed it at the back of the vignette.

"I'm not a gardener," Brooke says about the deep window boxes at the back of this room. "I don't know anything about plants," so when she asked Barbara Meyer to make the contents of the window boxes, she told her the flowers were iris, and sent her a photograph. "When she got the picture," Brooke laughs, "she phoned me and said, not only do you not know the difference between a rose and a carnation, you also don't know the difference between an iris and an orchid." What Brooke thought were iris turned out to be a bit more exotic. "There are 75 orchids in that little, tiny room," she declares, "a lot of them hidden down below."

One road leads to London...
—*John Masefield*

This room measures nine inches wide, is twelve inches tall, but is very deep — 15 to 18 inches, Brooke recalls, "a vignette, but it's deeper than most vignettes."

Brooke created the room, again "falling in love with the fabric when I saw it," to take with her on a seven-week sojourn in London in 1983, to show people an example of her work. "It's got an Old World look to it," she believes, "a sort of period piece. I didn't want to assault their eye," she explains. "I wanted to win them by doing something that they would want to look at."

And win them she did. During her stay in London Brooke was graciously received by one of the owners of Asprey & Company, a world-renowned dealer in fine art objects, exquisite jewelry, and important estate collections. She was escorted into Mr. Edward Asprey's office, she recalls, offered tea, and then "he spent 45 minutes with me, encouraging me."

The experience was repeated at Thomas Goode & Company, another very fine London establishment with similar merchandise, where Brooke was received by the Sales Director, a gentleman whose name had recently appeared on the Queen's List, and who spent an hour talking with Brooke. "They made me feel like a million dollars," she says, enthusiastically. "I came home with all kinds of good feelings about myself and my work."

This little vignette also appeared on the BBC, along with its creator, when Brooke was interviewed for a several-minute segment of a morning television news show.

She likes this room, she readily admits, "because it's the first time I broke with my own traditional style, and because of all the doors it opened for me, all the courtesy I was shown, the good things that happened to me because of it."

The little world of childhood with its familiar surroundings is a model of the greater world.
                                        —*Carl Gustav Jung*

*B*rooke envisions a little girl and her baby sister (or brother) sharing this charming room. Usually Brooke creates her nursery rooms in smaller vignettes, "but I had room to play in this one, and I really had a great time doing it."

The dollhouse, built into a wall, is an example of Brooke's attention to every possible detail. "I had a marvelous time with that dollhouse," Brooke remembers. "I painted all the backdrops, curtains, windows, and fireplace onto the walls."

The crib is Brooke's own design, one she teaches in a workshop, and uses quite often in her nursery rooms. "Sometimes, you know," she confides, "I'll design something and I'll like it so much I can't get away from it. I'll think, I did a good job and I like it, so why not use it again but in a different way?"

In this case, the crib is decorated with handpainted flowers to match the wallpaper, and the sides are silk gauze strung with ribbon.

"I had a lot of fun doing this room, with all the color combinations, the different patterns," Brooke says. And with the boxes, she might add. "This is a good example of my theory that everything is a box is a box is a box," she believes. "Everything you see in this room is an opening in a wall with a box behind it, containing something. The puppet stage is a box."

Above the little girl's bed are what at first glance appear to be framed pictures. They are actually one-inch square, framed boxes set into the wall with a figurine in each one.

A baby is an inestimable blessing...
—Mark Twain

"I wanted a romantic nursery," Brooke explains about this room. "I wanted it as delicate as possible." The soft colors and subtle floral prints of the wallpaper are carried through onto the woodwork and carpeting which Brooke has hand-painted. "I think that's the first time I ever painted a carpet," Brooke points out.

The planning of this room evolved from Brooke's philosophy that "in miniatures there should always be something more to discover. In some of my rooms, I hide things around a corner so that the viewer could look at it six times and still have something else to discover."

Behind the nursery, Brooke has "hidden" an entire garden scene with a perambulator under the shade of a tree, visible in a mirror over the changing table on the right of the room.

Royal Nursery

Brooke saw a photograph of this room in Ladies Home Journal magazine, and wanted to reproduce it in miniature because, she explains, "I'm an Anglophile and I was very excited" about the birth of a new prince.

As nearly as she could accomplish it, this room duplicates the Royal Nursery prepared for Prince William as it appeared in the magazine. It does not have the typical "Brooke" look because, she continues, "basically, everything does not match in this room."

The world is so full of a number
  of things,
I'm sure we should all be as
  happy as kings.
                    —*Robert Louis Stevenson*

"This is my favorite Christmas room," Brooke tells us, referring to the room pictured above. "I don't like 'gaudy,' and I don't think this is gaudy. I think this is just simple, New York penthouse elegance. That's exactly what I felt when I did it, and when I look at it now, I still have the same feeling.

"Whenever anyone asks me for the photographs representative of my work, this is one of the pictures I always send because I adore this room and I don't know why, but it's just. . .it's crisp, it's clean, it's neat, and it sparkles."

In this room, Brooke expanded on several techniques she first used in the Christmas vignette shown opposite. This has a similar use of mirrors and angled walls to make the Christmas tree the focal point. Balance is provided on the side walls by making the buffet nook and the bar opposite identical.

Behind the windows, Brooke has installed a New York city skyline scene. "I used it because that's the only place I could really envision this room," she explains, knowing that if it were possible, she would preside as hostess here, dressed in silver lamé.

Brooke's effective use of mirrors in this room includes the 1/4-inch squares she has used around and inside the buffet and bar, as well as on the dining tables. "I used them everywhere," she admits.

Style, elegance, drama, glamour — this room encompasses it all, a stunning example of the "Brooke" look!

Although she looks with a critical eye at her earlier work, as represented in the vignette shown opposite, Brooke says, "I always did like this room." It is the legs of the chairs that she feels are indicative of her early work because "my cabriole legs now are absolutely boney thin, very delicate." This vignette is owned by a fellow artisan in miniatures, which pleases Brooke very much because it indicates to her praise from her peers. "When one of my contemporaries buys my work, it's such an honor," Brooke believes. "It's really a compliment."

At Christmas play, and make good cheer, For Christmas comes but once a year.
—*Thomas Tusser*

This elegant, stylized black and white kitchen would delight any gourmet cook. Color accents are provided by the red geraniums and the shiny copper pots.

When Brooke spotted the family of black and white spaniels (seen in the photo at right) made by Gail Morey, the idea for the entire room came to her mind.

The kitchen Brooke envisioned had black and white tiles, some with geraniums in the center of each one. Joe Hermes, who produces a variety of tile patterns for miniaturists, "reworked his Venetian tile for me," Brooke explains, putting in just the borders and printing black pots in some of them. Larger tiles with the border pattern only were used on the floor of the kitchen. For the counter top and around the cooking surface, Brooke hand-painted red geraniums with green leaves over the pot designs, then used several coats of Deft finish, polishing between each coat, before cutting the tiles apart to install them. "Then I grouted them and Defted them again," she says. "There is a lot of procedure in that tile work."

An unabashed Anglophile and avid reader,

...Brooke remembers a library in the Tucker home during her very young years. "I mean a *whole* room that was a real library," she says with the reverence of one who has loved books all her life. "When I was a baby," she recalls her mother telling her later, "just crawling around and pulling myself up, I would find this one particular book among these hundreds of books, no matter where she put it. It was the only book I wanted. She told me," Brooke continues, "how she used to come in and find me, sitting on the floor, with my face in that book, smelling it."

The book, printed in England, bound in red leather, stamped in gold, and lined with silk, is about King Edward VII and his Queen, Alexandra, one of Brooke's favorites, it turns out, among England's Queens. "When I moved in here," she explains, "they had a housewarming for me, and this was my mother's housewarming gift. This book," she says, amazed, "after all those years."

Brooke's own library has grown to include hundreds of books, as well as other memorabilia relating to the English Royal Family. She has almost as many books in her collection about Imperial Russia, the last Czars, and their favorite jeweler, Carl Faberge.

Immersing herself in these historical times, Brooke often wonders about reincarnation. Only half in jest, she says, "I think I must have been born into an aristocratic family, or an Imperial one," insisting that "I put on airs all the time."

Brooke's ongoing passion for books and reading found expression in this two-story, panelled library which is shown in color on page 57. This is one of the basic rooms that she teaches in her workshops.

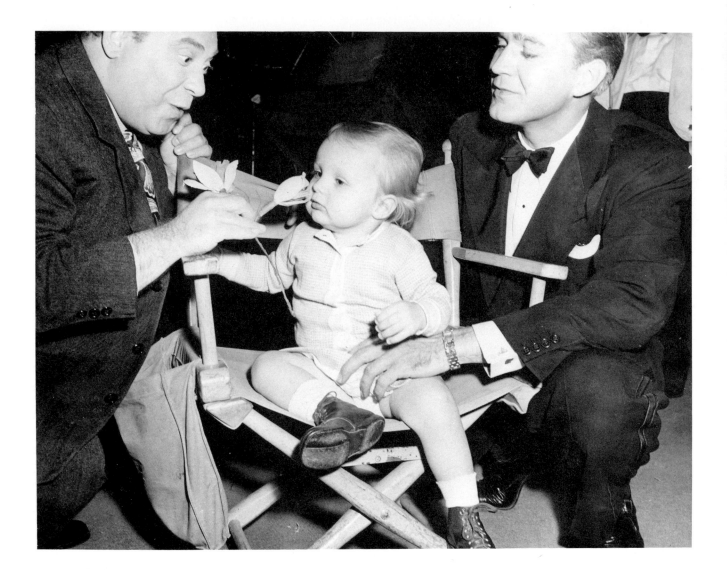

When Brooke was born, she had an orthopedic problem that required some surgery followed by braces and casts, and then corrective shoes.

For a few years while she was a toddler, Brooke says, ''I had to wear these ugly, brown, lace-up shoes. ''It got to be an expensive proposition because,'' she relates, ''you know how children's feet grow.''

Brooke's mother would buy the brown shoes and take them to a cobbler who cut open the soles, inserted steel plates, and sewed them up again.

It was a treat when Brooke was allowed to wear a pair of pretty, party shoes when, for example, she was to be photographed with her famous father. It was on one of those occasions that this photograph was taken.

Her mother had dressed Brooke in a pretty dress and bonnet, but forgot to change the brown, lace-up shoes. Brooke had been brought to the set where her father was working, cameras were there to record the event, and the photographs later appeared in a movie magazine. ''My mother was mortified when the photographs appeared,'' Brooke says, ''She thought, what must people think; we're dressing our child in patched shoes.''

Now, years later, Brooke has what she calls a fetish about shoes, and owns 120 pair. ''My biggest treat in life,'' she laughs, ''is to be able to go out and buy new shoes.'' She keeps them in boxes, labeled and stacked in her closet. Sometimes, she says, when she is looking for a pair of shoes to wear, ''it's like going shopping in my own closet.''

When this book was in the planning stages, no one was more pleased and excited about it than ''Nana,'' Brooke's grandmother. Emily Jolley, now 85 years young, is an important part of Brooke's life and her career. ''She's helped me enormously in a lot of different ways,'' Brooke says emphatically.

Emily and her husband, I. Stanford Jolley, moved their family of four to California during the Depression years. Mr. Jolley, Brooke called him ''Pop-pop,'' became a renowned character actor who appeared in more than 500 films over the years. Although he played the ''steely-eyed villain'' in most of his films, Brooke says she has ''never known a man in my life who was kinder to people than my grandfather was.'' Mr. Jolley, who died in 1979, is fondly remembered in the entertainment industry.

When the Jolleys first came to California Emily took a job in the sewing room at RKO Studios where she worked intermittently for many years on elaborate costumes worn by the movie stars of those days, including the famous Deanna Durbin wedding gown. ''She has stories to tell,'' Brooke continues, ''about the billions of sequins she has sewn on by hand.

''She's got a great eye for fashion,'' Brooke believes, ''to this day. My mother and I both benefited from Nana's making our clothes.'' Emily sewed and altered Brooke's wardrobe until just recently when her eyesight began to fail. She also helped with ''my accessory line,'' Brooke says, the smaller items Brooke sells at shows in addition to her rooms.

''After Pop-pop died,'' Brooke explains, ''Nana and I just grew closer and closer together. We share a common sense of humor about a lot of things, and I talk to her every day on the phone.''

And so, a special toast to ''Nana,'' with love from Brooke. ''A super neat lady,'' Brooke believes. ''How we've grown together!''

Open and outgoing, warm and generous, Brooke's friends describe her. Dynamic, energetic, with an unfailing sense of humor and a special zest for life, they all agree. To Mary McLune, owner of the Mini-Bazaar shop in Newport Beach, California, Brooke is "a very dear and loyal friend. I have great respect and admiration for her as a person, and as an artist."

Both Mary and Annette Gupman, another friend of Brooke's and also a miniaturist, have known Brooke since she first started creating miniature rooms over a dozen years ago. Annette recalls the day she met Brooke at the Miniken Fantasies Shop. "Brooke came in with a room she had made and it was exciting, something really different and new." They began an ongoing friendship that very day.

"I don't know if people realize how many times she has made a room and donated it," Annette says about Brooke's penchant for helping with a variety of fundraisers in her own special way. "That's the kind of person she is."

Her close friend of almost twenty years, Sherry Van Woensel, knows Brooke as a caring as well as generous person. "She's one of those people who no matter how busy she might be, if I called and said I needed her, she'd be there," Sherry states simply, adding that Brooke cannot pass an injured animal on the street. Where most of us might go on by and call to report it, Brooke stops her car, tries to locate the owner, and if she cannot, takes the animal to a vet herself. "I've known her to do this often," Sherry explains, adding that she has been a passenger in Brooke's car many times.

Although Brooke's driving habits are more subdued these days, Sherry remembers thinking at one time that Brooke "must have taken driving lessons from a New York cabdriver." Recalling an incident that happened one day when the two were on their way to a garage sale, Sherry laughs, "Brooke made one of those lurching stops, right next to a phone booth which happened to be occupied. The woman inside dropped the phone, threw up her hands, and ran."

Clearly, Brooke's guardian angel, whom she calls Homer Finkle, was watching over her that

Thousands of hours of creativity have taken place in this room.

day, as he usually does. "If she is in a bad situation," Sherry says, "she calls on Homer and he always comes through."

To supplement Homer's assistance, Brooke makes wishes. "Ever since I was a small child," Brooke confides, "I have never knowingly passed a body of water without stopping, throwing in some pennies, and making wishes."

Homer may have been on hand the day Brooke's work table was installed in her apartment. Built by Sherry's husband Jerry, the sturdy table seemed too large to go through the door to the room for which it was intended. She and Brooke "tried it every which way," Sherry recalls, "and it wouldn't go." What to do? "Well, we decided to sit down and have a glass of wine," Sherry continues, amused, "and when we tried it again, we got that table in there. I don't know how."

The table is still in her work room, along with supplies of all kinds, on shelves of all descriptions, accessories in hundreds of labeled drawers, source books neatly arranged, and a closet packed full of fabrics and wallpaper. Thousands of hours of creativity have taken place in this room.

Because she often works up to 17 hours a day at her own craft, Brooke has a great respect for other artists of all persuasions. "She inspires other people," Annette explains, "and uses the work of many other artisans in her rooms." "It's astronomical," Mary adds, "the number of quality items she puts in a room."

Brooke feels it is important to include the work of her gifted contemporaries, she says, because "collectors are very knowledgeable now," and can recognize the work of many of today's artisans. "If they buy one of my rooms," she explains, "they know they are buying other artisans' work within that room. This is how we help each other grow," Brooke adds.

It might not be necessary to use such an extraordinary number of quality items in each of her rooms to achieve the effect she wants, but she does it. That's the kind of person she is.

Brooke Tucker has a presence, a "star" quality, her friends agree. "Her magnetic personality always seems to draw a crowd," Mary McLune believes. Some years ago, Annette Gupman recalls, both she and Mary watched fondly as people approached Brooke at miniature shows, somewhat in awe of her, asking, "Are you really Brooke Tucker?"

Annette decided it would be amusing to start a Brooke Tucker Fan Club, so she designed a membership card, began taking names, and collected the 38 cents decided upon as a membership fee, although the cards themselves cost her more than that. "I was being facetious," Annette admits, laughing, teasing her good friend. But the idea proved so popular that Annette now has a book of "members" numbering into the thousands.

Beauty is in the eye of the beholder.
—Margaret Wolfe Hungerford

Not every work of art elicits a positive response from every person who sees it, and Brooke Tucker's rooms are no exception.

Brooke had created a Christmas room in white with red and green some time ago and had it for sale at a N.A.M.E. Regional Houseparty in a western city. Late one afternoon she was sitting behind her display table, out of sight, when she overheard two women talking about the room.

Did you ever see anything so ugly in your whole life?'' Brooke recalls one woman asking other, who replied, as nearly as Brooke can remember now, that it was the worst Christmas room she had ever seen. Brooke sat quietly, not willing to embarrass the two women by letting them know she overheard their cutting remarks.

Early the next morning, Brooke continues, ''a woman walked up to me and she really almost had tears in her eyes. She took my hand and said, 'I have something to tell you,' '' Brooke recalls now with amusement, adding, ''I thought, she's going to tell me this is so bad it made her cry.''

But the woman who held Brooke's hand wanted to tell her that she would buy the room, and to tell her why. Brooke remembers that the woman told her that she had stood in front of the room, looking at it, for quite some time the day before, ''and I had seen her,'' Brooke continues. ''The

woman said, 'I went back to my hotel room last night and I couldn't forget about that room. I thought it was the loveliest thing I had ever seen in my life.' ''

As Brooke recalls the conversation, the woman told her she called her daughter, long distance, to tell her about Brooke's room. The daughter thought her mother should buy it if she liked it that much. The woman had not considered that a possibility because, as she told Brooke, she had worked much of her life, had just retired, and was more accustomed to saving her money for retirement.

''And she told me,'' Brooke says, '' 'I hesitated on the phone, thinking for the first time, I can buy it, I can really buy it.' Well,'' Brooke continues, ''it was such a lovely feeling for me because, on the one hand were these two women who hated the room, and here was a woman who could not believe she was going to own the very same room *she* thought was so beautiful.

''It's all in the eye of the beholder,'' Brooke adds, ending the story.

This is not the same Christmas room mentioned above, but is one of many Brooke has created over the years. She prefers her Christmas rooms to have ''a simple elegance,'' she says. '' 'Messy' Christmases are charming, but I can't live in that kind of chaos.''

A dozen years ago, shortly after Brooke discovered miniatures, she took a class in the creation of a miniature room, taught by Laura Davis at Beehive Studio near Chicago. One of the lessons Laura taught her was to look at her work with the critical eye of a "nosy neighbor."

Each of us knows such a person, Brooke believes. "She's the person who will find all the mistakes you don't want her to see, and she'll point them out to you in the sweetest way," she says, sarcastically. "She wishes she could do what you're doing, but she can't. There's really nothing she can criticize so she looks for the tiniest detail to mention."

To keep the "nosy neighbor" quiet, Brooke say, "you carry through, you follow around a corner, you finish things off. I always work with an eye to what the 'nosy neighbor' might see."

These two vignettes in glass cases are prototype examples of one of the most popular workshops Brooke conducts all over the country. Both rooms are essentially alike in dimension and layout, but each shows how different the same spaces can be made to appear.

Successful
interior design

...as we can clearly see, is vibrant and viable, a versatile art form encompassing a variety of themes.

As a professional designer Brooke is equally as versatile working with a masculine theme as she is with any other. In fact, Brooke admits she "loves to do masculine rooms." She believes that the various facets of one's personality come into play in the design process, allowing her to work as easily in a masculine theme as she does in a feminine one, for instance.

On the following pages are some of Brooke's favorite rooms with masculine themes. In many cases they incorporate the boldest examples we will see of her use of color, texture and form.

Good friends, good books and a sleepy conscience: This is the ideal life.

—Mark Twain

"This was the room that inspired the panel library workshop I teach," Brooke explains. "I teach the basic unfinished room and the students do what they want to it, as I did."

Admitting that "I could very well have this room in my own house," Brooke describes its atmosphere as "warm." The walls and floor are cherry veneer to which she has added inlay strips for contrast and detail.

The theme of this room, the hunt, is one of Brooke's favorites for masculine rooms. "I have used the hunt theme in various ways because it denotes the aristocracy," Brooke says, adding, "and I love aristocratic things."

This room is one and a half stories including the mezzanine level where the bookcases are built into the wall. Below that is a cozy fireplace area with a card table and two comfortable chairs in front.

"This is the study of the master of the hounds," Brooke explains, telling the story of what is going on in the room. "His boots and riding crop are by the staircase, and his hat is hanging on the newel post. He and a friend are playing cards and having a hot toddy after the hunt."

The carpeting in the foreground is a tapestry that Brooke describes as one of her favorites. "I've used it quite a lot," she admits, "because I happen to like it. It's dramatic."

Although they were created at different times, the tapestry carpeting in this room is the same one Brooke used in the library shown just before. And, the ceiling treatment in that library is used as a wallpaper in this room.

"I had a marvelous time doing this room," Brooke comments. The room was a commission to her, but not a copy of any particular room. "It came out of my head," she says.

This game/living/dining room combination is thirty inches wide, one of the largest spaces Brooke works in. The use of mirrors expands the space even further.

"That plaid mirror which you can see in the dining room picture comes in 12-inch squares," Brooke explains. "I bought boxes of it when it first came out, in case it was discontinued, and it was." Brooke re-cut the glass, using it in strips, piecing it together like a puzzle, to get the even look she wanted.

There is a great deal of activity suggested in this room, with the pool table, a chess game set up, "and people expected for dinner," Brooke explains, pointing out the gold service on the dining room table.

"That table was a real challenge," she recalls. Brooke hand cut strips of brass, mitered the corners, and inlaid them into the wood of the table top.

The less of routine, the more of life.

—*A.B. Alcott*

Art is the desire of a man to express himself, to record the reactions of his personality to the world he lives in.

—*Amy Lowell*

This room was selected from hundreds of contest entries to appear on the cover of the 1986 Calendar published by the miniatures magazine, Nutshell News. Created in 1985, it was a commissioned room in which Brooke incorporated many of the interests of its owner, a Catholic priest.

One of the challenges to Brooke in creating this masculine study was to find suitable paintings that would reflect the priest's major interest, the church. "I wanted fine, tasteful religious art," she emphasizes, "not anything overly senti-mental." In her search she turned to a favorite resource — a huge set of catalogs of art prints purchased years ago. Pouring over them, she found several religious paintings by the Old Masters that she felt were suitable in both reverence and artistic sophistication.

At *her request, the priest sent Brooke a list of his likes and dislikes, but the room is an original, not a copy of any existing room. "The list of 'likes' provides valuable guidelines for me," Brooke explains, "but the 'dislikes' are even more important. If I include something in a room that the customer hates, he'll be turned off by the entire room."*

One of the items on the owner of this room's "likes" list was the expression, "Have a rainbow day," which he associates with the rainbow given by God as a sign to Noah and all mankind of his promise never again to destroy the earth by flood. On the right wall, next to the bar, can be seen a painting of Noah's Ark with a rainbow.

It is the close observation of little things which is the secret of success in business, in art, in science, and in every pursuit of life.

—*Samuel Smiles*

"I *LOVE* this room," Brooke exclaims. "*Of all the masculine rooms I have ever done, this is my favorite!*"

Using basically the same layout as the paneled library, again one and a half stories tall, Brooke succeeded in achieving an entirely different look. The room idea came from a Ralph Lauren advertisement Brooke saw in a magazine. She recalls that the photograph included a brass bed, a chair with a riding habit and a lap robe arranged on it and a pair of boots nearby.

"*It took me so long to find these fabrics,*" *she recalls.* "*I searched high and low for the little pieces of fabric I needed to make that bed look like the Ralph Lauren ad. And I'm so thrilled with this room,*" *she adds, smiling.*

Genius is the ability to reduce the
complicated to the simple.
—*C.W. Ceram*

Polka dot and plaid silk fabrics combine elegantly in this masculine room done in navy and shades of brown. But it is the wall treatment that seems to first catch the viewer's eye.

Brook constructs the walls in sections before installing them into the room. For the wall treatment in this room, she says, "I cut strips of brass, cork, wood, silk, all kinds of things, and put them in a pile next to me." Then, with the wall section laid flat on her work table, "I just started cutting and laying with no particular thought in mind of design, just putting on strips and gluing until the wall was filled." She used this technique above the fireplace as well as in the corner behind the bar. Pleased with the result, Brook says, "it's dramatic and it's different."

Another commission, Brooke envisioned this room in the home of a "wealthy, Southern gentleman who doesn't happen to be married, and who has a very elegant place." It is obvious that the stories about the inhabitants of many of her rooms are an integral part of the room itself, starting with the planning process.

In this case, the "owner's" portrait hangs over the fireplace. Brooke cut the picture from the magazine advertisement of a portrait studio. "The minute I knew I was going to do this room, I knew what picture I was going to use," she recalls. "He really looks as though he lives in this room."

At the opposite side of this large room, in the dining area, a mural handpainted especially for Brooke by Mountaintop Miniatures is the focal point.

The black woodwork in this room provides elegant continuity, tying together the bold colors and textures Brooke has combined here. "I went through fits trying to get a nice, black finish," she laughs, "without it having a patent leather look." After considerable experimentation, she settled on black shoe polish and Deft finish, "and

it worked beautifully," she says, satisfied with the results.

Brooke's flair for the dramatic is especially evident in this masculine room with its vivid color and design combinations. Choosing the right ones, she feels, is more difficult than it is in other types of rooms. "You can make anything into a pretty bedroom," Brooke believes, "if you use the right color combinations, but you cannot make just anything into a really luxurious masculine room, at least I can't."

The first rule of decoration is that you can break almost all the other rules.

—Billy Baldwin

Brooke accepts commissions as time permits, but "if customers want me to copy a room, they have to give me license to copy it my own way, and to the best of my ability," she explains.

There were two things that especially excited her about doing this room, Brooke confides: the bathroom with its unique sink and handpainted motif on the cupboard doors, and the variety of furniture styles incorporated into the bedroom area. "All those different cabriole legs," Brooke laughs. "That excited me. Now I want to go around putting cabriole legs on everything!"

The project took longer than Brooke anticipated "because there was so much that I had to learn to do." Among the techniques she perfected was the "faux marbre" of the bathroom countertop and floor. She constructed and hand-painted the sink to exactly duplicate the real one, using the manufacturer's catalog photographs as her guide.

(Smaller pictures on these pages show original, full-size room.)

Hand-painting on the closet doors, as
well as the latticework detailing above
the bathtub, was done in a slightly
darker color than in the full-size
room because Brooke wanted "to
make it more vivid, to get some
contrast."

In the real-size room there are more accessories than could be used in its miniature counterpart without it having a cluttered look. "You try to be faithful to the room you are copying," Brooke explains, "but I still wanted to create my own look. When I make a room I tend to have every accessory melt into the room."

The accessories used on the mantel convey the feeling of the full-size room effectively, yet do not overwhelm the miniature scene. Brooke hand-painted each of the accessories used here.

Domes like this one have been very popular with Brooke's customers. She calls them "a moment in time." Although the dome space is small, Brooke says, "I try to get as much into it as I can."

This dome features a serving table at the front, built in a semi-circle to fit the space, and a table and two chairs. The window in the back has a stained glass design, an iris similar to the ones in the wallpaper pattern. "What I was trying to do," Brooke explains, "is pick up the pattern from the wallpaper in a big, but soft, splash of color."

A Moment in Time

Some of the people who collect Brooke's work prefer smaller pieces. "I do them to give my customers variety," she explains. These smaller pieces are often lamps or domes. Examples of both are shown here. "I've done quite a few of them," Brooke says. The themes are similar to ones she uses in her rooms, but show only a corner of the visualized scene, or "a moment in time," as she explains it.

Working in a smaller space takes as much planning and ingenuity as working in a larger one. Often the furniture used must conform to the outside parameters, i.e. the semi-circular serving table in one dome and the tufted bench of the same shape in another.

Each of these pieces is meant to be viewed from several vantage points and each has the unmistakable "Brooke look."

Style
Balance
Harmony
Drama

The masculine room (above left) is an example of Brooke's early work. What she wanted to achieve here was something rather dramatic, and so she placed birdcages on either side of the fireplace. Another early work, the country living room pictured at left, donated to raise money for the National Association of Miniature Enthusiasts, came into Brooke's head when she found the ceramic chicken on the table in front of the couch. The fireplace (above), although miniature, could just as easily be a model for a real-size living room or library, illustrating that style, balance and harmony are key assets to an interior decorator in any scale.

Elegant bridal bedrooms like the one pictured above are often a favorite theme of Brooke's. "They're really just feminine bedrooms," Brooke claims, "but I have used the bridal theme quite frequently." This one is a good example of the sophisticated lighting Brooke uses to create the effect she wants. The room was meant to be set into a wall and viewed as one would a painting. Lighting behind the window at the rear adds further depth and interest to the whole room.

Not a breeze or a stray leaf blows into Brooke's patio scenes, and yet the rooms invite the viewer in for a beverage or a meal. The patio at left, contemporary and stylized, has the characteristic crispness typical of Brooke's work.

"I'll never do a house"...

...Brooke had breezily announced on many occasions. When she finally did, the project had all the drama, excitement, and even the longevity, of a very successful Broadway show.

In 1983 she received a phone call at her Burbank apartment. It was from a woman who said she was the personal secretary to a family who lived in the Southwest, and who owned a number of Brooke's miniature rooms. "This family had been buying my rooms for several years," Brooke later found out, "and they finally got in touch with me because the 12-year-old daughter wanted to meet me." When, the secretary wanted to know, could they fly to Los Angeles to meet Brooke?

On the appointed day, a long black limousine slid into the tiny parking space outside Brooke's building. Two men, dressed in black, waited by the car while the rest of the group filed up the stairs and into the small apartment. "My room filled up," Brooke recalls. "There was the mother, the daughter, the grandfather, the astrologer, the secretary, the accountant, the governess — I don't know," she says incredulously, counting on her fingers. "They had come here to meet me, and brought a retinue of 15 people!"

The purpose of the visit soon became clear. The little girl's mother had bought a miniature house from the wife of an ex-president of a South American country, a copy of the woman's former home. "We want you to come and do this house," Brooke recalls being told.

Not possible, Brooke tried to explain. "First of all, I don't do other people's work, and second, I'm not into houses." As she recalls the conversation, Brooke says, "I said if I ever worked on a house, it would have to be in my own mind. I would have to design it. But my schedule is really heavy right now. I have teaching commitments, shows and other room orders to do." Without persuading Brooke to take on the project, the group left to spend the night in a luxurious Beverly Hills hotel.

The next day, a phone call. You must think about doing the house, Brooke was urged. In a way, she already was; ideas were beginning to form in her mind. "So I got together with a couple of my real good friends,'' Brooke says, ''and we talked about it.'' Argued might be a better word. Her friends urged her to take on the project even though it would involve up to a year of Brooke's time. The financial arrangements would allow her to stay at home, concentrating on this one project, while giving up shows and workshops for the duration. ''But it's just like the movie business,'' Brooke explains. ''You stay away from the public too long and nobody's even going to know you.'' A difficult decision had to be made.

In the end it was the challenge of the project, the satisfaction of creating something of this size (the completed house would be 13-1/2 feet long) that caused Brooke to accept.

Claiming that she knew nothing about houses, Brooke says, ''I do rooms and there's a big difference. People don't usually understand that.'' She conceived in her mind a house that would be a series of rooms and contacted a family friend, Marvin Davis. ''He's a very fine architect,'' she says, ''who designed part of Disneyland. He did the blueprints and they are just beautiful.''

Brooke decided the house would have a bridal theme, ''the day of the wedding, and it would have the kind of rooms that normally go into a miniature house,'' she explains, ''a baby's room, a child's room, the young girl's room, the parents' room, so I could use different accessories and so forth.'' Yellow roses would decorate the main rooms of the house, because ''the wedding reception is going to be held here,'' Brooke continues her story, ''so it would give me a reason for the theme to be carried throughout the house.''

Brooke was well into the construction of the first series of rooms, each of which was designed to slide into its niche in the main structure, when the project encountered its first serious prob-

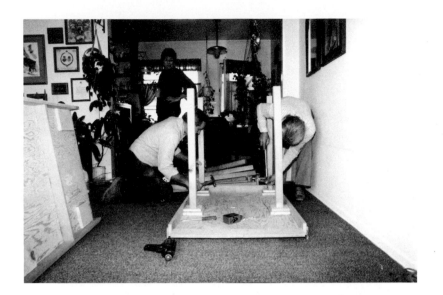

lem. The original commission for the house might have to be canceled.

After several uncertain months, Brooke found out that it would be. "I had canceled an entire year of my life," she explains, not at all calmly. "I had no time to re-book the shows because I had nothing prepared to take to a show. And you can't re-schedule classes at the drop of a hat. Classes take three or four months to work up to," she says. "If it hadn't been for my really close friends, who helped me financially and in every possible way they could," Brooke says, her voice husky with emotion, "I could not have survived this period."

What to do? "I had to sell this house," Brooke decided; "not room by room, the house wasn't designed that way." Reluctantly, because "I don't like to promote my own work like that; it makes me nervous," Brooke phoned a few of the people who had bought her rooms in the past. "I said, maybe you can spread the word that it's available," she recalls. It wasn't long before the dollhouse had a new owner.

Brooke again turned her full attention to the project, and another serious problem arose, this time with the basic construction of the shell itself. Working in the center section of the house, Brooke says, "I started fitting the stairs and just nothing was right." The stairs had been built of cherry from the original blueprints, Brooke says, "by John Haight, and they are so gorgeous, and should have fit perfectly." The shell, it seemed, had not been constructed properly, was not reinforced as it should have been, and had warped out of shape.

Discouraged, Brooke asked her friend and fellow miniatures artisan, Derek Perkins, to assess the situation. "He's very methodical, a very fine craftsman," she believes. Derek could instantly see the problem Brooke had encountered

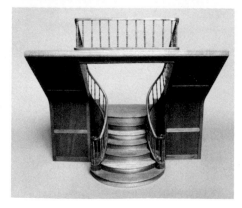

and could foresee future ones if she continued working on the structure as it was. Moreover, he agreed to help her correct it.

"I simply would not have a house without Derek Perkins," Brooke says with conviction. "It's the expertise. He's very accurate where I'm more creative, more abstract." The center section of the house went to Derek's workshop for considerable rebuilding, the application of stonework to the outside, and the installation of handcrafted windows.

In the meantime, Brooke continued with other phases of the project, including the construction of almost all the furniture for the house, some of which involved techniques she had never used before.

Although the four bedrooms in the house each has its own decor, the dining room, living room and three-story main hall has a unified decorating scheme based on a blue and beige striped fabric from Vienna that Brooke has used in several different ways.

"That was the hardest thing for me to do," Brooke believes. "Because I create individual rooms, I'm not used to continuity, and I had to work with the same fabric, the same color scheme, in what is actually five rooms."

Continuity, too, appears in the decorations for the wedding. From the white Rolls Royce near the front door which Brooke has decorated with yellow roses and ribbon, these flowers can be seen in each of the main rooms of the house, in table arrangements and on the wedding cake in the dining room.

Beyond the dining room with its horseshoe table laden with elegant refreshments on gold plates, the wedding guests might wander out to the patio through a charming blue and white kitchen which Brooke concedes was an after-thought. "When the house was built, I forgot to put in a kitchen because I don't cook," she confesses.

Arnell Manor's two elegant center halls owe their majestic sweep and classical elegance to John Haight's magnificent stairs, built from cherry from the original blueprints.

Although the kitchen is by far the smallest space in this house, it is nonetheless an inviting, efficient nook. "I was quite pleased with the way it came out," Brooke admits.

A separate structure on the far side of the patio was built as a retreat for Brooke's mythical father of the bride, with "my two favorite rooms," Brooke confesses. "Technically, I think I did my best work in these rooms." The lower room, built on two levels, contains a double fireplace.

The upstairs room's color scheme coordinates with the lower one and here Brooke has used accessories that would personalize the room for the owner. "The painting near the pool table," she explains, "is the same one he has hanging in his real study."

Brooke worked on this project, her first house, over a three-year period. When it was finally completed, each room in its niche and perfectly lighted, the landscaping in place, and the table under the house skirted in white, Brooke held an open house.

It was gloomy and overcast the day her completed house was to be viewed for the first time. "My favorite kind of day," Brooke laughs. The house, its lights the only ones in the room, sat against one long wall in her living room. Her guests were due to arrive in an hour.

"For the first time I sat quietly across the room, and looked at the house," Brooke recalls. "I've rarely been able to do this, but that day I actually put myself in that car, in my mind. Then I got out of the car and walked through the front door. As I walked through the living room, I checked to make sure everything was in place. I was being a hostess in this house," Brooke says simply.

"I walked through the entire house as a small person, and it was the strangest sensation. But it was a real thrill."

It had been many, many months of highs and lows, of problems met and solved, of talents offered and accepted, of techniques tried and perfected, and especially of friendships formed and cherished. "You cannot believe the support I've had from so many people on this house," Brooke emphasizes. "Without that I don't think I could have gotten it done. There are so many fine artisans represented," she continues, "it would be impossible to list them all."

But, in the final analysis, the house is a Brooke Tucker Original, and one of which she can be justly proud. Enjoy your tour of it.

Thirteen and a half feet long, the completed house, "The Yellow Rose of Texas," awaits the wedding festivities in elegant splendor.

The Living Room

The woodwork in this room, and throughout the main rooms of the house, is cherry. All of these areas share a common color scheme based on a blue and beige striped fabric from Vienna that Brooke has used in several different ways.

"That was the hardest thing for me to do," Brooke believes. "Because I do individual rooms, I'm not used to continuity, and I had to work with the same fabric, the same color scheme in what is really five rooms."

Brooke used the Viennese striped fabric in the living room as part of the window treatment and to upholster a pair of cherry arm chairs. The same fabric is also used above the room's well-stocked bar.

The Dining Room

Off the center hall on the left, the dining room has been prepared for the wedding reception with a horseshoe-shaped table laden with gold plates of food. Commenting on the special architectural effects she created on the back wall, Brooke says, "I wanted something different and unusual, so I just started cutting arches. Then after I had all these arches, I didn't know what to do with them," she recalls with amusement. "I had to come up with a piece of furniture that had an arch to it." The resulting cabinet, filled with gold service plates, became the focal point of the room.

I sing. . .of bridegrooms, brides, and of their bridal cakes.
                    —*Robert Herrick*

The Kitchen

Although the kitchen in this house is quite small, it is filled with charming details, accessories repeating the blue and white color scheme, and a latticed window. "When the house was built, I forgot to put in a kitchen," Brooke confides, adding that "I don't cook. I can't stand doing that kind of stuff." In spite of its being an afterthought, the kitchen is a delightful blend of practicality and Brooke's flair for the dramatic.

The Patio

Wedding guests might wander through the kitchen to an attractive patio filled with plants and wicker furniture Brooke has covered to coordinate with the striped awnings along the back wall. Although they are not visible, there are copper pennies in the fountain in the center of this room, ''for luck,'' Brooke confides.

Two-story Retreat

When Brooke began making plans for the house, she realized that it would necessarily be a feminine house because of the theme she had chosen. But since she feels that some of her best rooms are those with a masculine theme, she decided to create a two-story retreat for the father of the bride. They are her "two favorite rooms," she confides. "Technically, I think I did my best work in these rooms."

The lower room, built on two levels, contains a double fireplace, a technique that is difficult to accomplish. "The second fireplace, on the mezzanine level, can only be viewed from the

mirror behind the desk," Brooke explains. A painting of Windsor Castle hangs above the fireplace, while a large mural of an English country scene fills the overmantle of the lower one.

The upstairs room has a color scheme similar to the one below it for continuity, but, Brooke explains, "I was trying for different textures and odd shapes." The chess table, she says, "was a real challenge for me, to design it, to figure out how to make it." She shaped the table out of poster board, then covered it with cherry veneer. "Then I inlaid the top of the table in strips of cherry," Brooke continues, "and inlaid the chess board in the center, so it's all a flat surface."

The Parents' Bedroom

Of the flower print fabric she used as a
bedspread, around the windows, and to upholster
the sofa, Brooke says, "I loved that fabric when
I saw it. That's how most of my rooms come to
be; I'll see a piece of fabric and I'll just 'know'
the room."

Brooke is especially pleased with this
photograph (showing the fireplace) because the
architectural details shown make it look so much
like a full-size room.

The parents' bedroom is the only room that Brooke has created with two bathrooms, each decorated with one of the two fabrics used in the bedroom. Typically, neither room contains a toilet. Taken as a whole, the rooms are an excellent example of how Brooke coordinates adjoining spaces.

The Bride's Bedroom

The oldest child in the mythical family Brooke envisioned for the dollhouse is about to become a bride. Brooke appliqued the wedding dress, adding seed pearls to it. The dress can be seen hanging on the closet door.

Focal points in this room are the soft pastel mural Brooke commissioned for the back wall, and a delicate, airy canopied bed. Here again, Brooke combines the bridal theme with a profusion of pink roses. An elegant bathroom is part of this suite.

**A thousand fantasies begin to throng
into my memory.**

—John Milton

The Twins' Room

Twins, a boy and a girl, occupy this charming child's room. Brooke has used pink and blue as the color scheme, incorporating her favorite pink roses on the girl's side of the room, and using a blue and white stripe on the boy's side. The picket fence motif effectively ties the two together.

The Nursery

Sunny yellows and crisp greens are combined in the room the baby in Brooke's mythical dollhouse family shares with Nanny. Brooke points out the sewing nook where, she says, "Nanny is making a dress for the baby." A skirted table in front of the fireplace is set for afternoon tea.

The decorative panels on the walls are gift wrap paper Brooke made a special call to the manufacturer to get when she could not find enough to use. "I called," she says, "and told them I must have more of this stuff. It was in the stores, but it wasn't being produced anymore." The secretary Brooke talked with found a roll and sent it to her. "I was very dramatic on the phone," Brooke continues, laughing; "I think she thought I would commit suicide or something if I didn't find it."